NATIONAL GEOGRAPHIC

my first Pocket Guide

W9-CEN-727

ROCKS

AND

MINERALS

DR. PAUL M. A. WILLIS

**NATIONAL
GEOGRAPHIC
SOCIETY**

INTRODUCTION

Rocks and minerals are everywhere around you. They form the earth beneath your feet and most of the buildings you visit. Many things you use every day began as rocks. All metal objects, such as knives and forks, scissors, cars, trains, and planes come from rocks. Bricks and glass do, too. The coal that we burn to make electricity is a rock. So you can see how important rocks are.

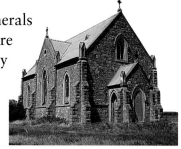

There are many different kinds of rocks, but they are all made of different types of minerals or small bits of other rocks.

Each type of rock and every mineral has its own special features. If you learn about some of these features, you will soon be able to identify the rocks you find and the minerals they contain.

Rock collecting is an interesting and easy hobby. You don't have to chase rocks, and you won't have to feed them once they are in your collection! Many rocks and minerals have beautiful colors or patterns and make great displays.

HOW TO USE THIS BOOK

Each spread in this book describes one rock or mineral. A shaded map in "Where To Find" shows where you can find the rock or mineral. "What To Look For" lists features, such as color and shape, that will help you identify it. Learn a new fact in the "Field Notes," and see exactly what the rock or mineral looks like in the photograph. For each mineral, a diagram shows the shape of its crystals. For each rock, a drawing of a magnifying glass shows the detail of its grains. If you come across a word you do not know, look it up in the Glossary on page 76.

HOW ROCKS ARE MADE

You will enjoy rock collecting more if you understand some things about rocks and minerals. What are they made of? Where did they come from? Rocks tell us about the past, about the time before there were any people. With patience and a little practice, you will soon learn some fascinating facts about the earth.

There are three groups of rocks: igneous (IG-nee-us), sedimentary (sed-uh-MEN-tuh-ree), and metamorphic (met-uh-MOR-fik). Each group is formed in different ways.

Igneous rocks form from magma, rock that has been heated deep in the earth until it melts into a red, superhot liquid.

Magma that flows from a volcano is called lava.

The magma flows through cracks in the earth and may stay deep underground or break through to the surface. When it cools, the magma turns into solid rock—with large crystals if it is inside the earth or small crystals if it is on the surface.

You can see bits of other rocks in this sedimentary rock.

Old rocks can be broken down by wind and rain into sediments such as mud, sand, or gravel. Most sedimentary rocks form when sediments settle on the bottom of oceans or rivers and are cemented together by minerals in the water. A few sedimentary rocks, such as coal, come from decayed plants that turn into minerals over time.

Metamorphic rocks are rocks that have changed because they have been heated, or because they have been squeezed by movements in the earth—or both.

This is a metamorphic rock called slate. It formed from shale that was squeezed during mountain building.

LOOKING AT MINERALS

M inerals are the building blocks of all rocks. There are hundreds of different minerals. Some of the more common ones are shown in this book.

Olivine can look like green glass.

A mineral can be as big as a person, but most minerals are tiny. You will need a good magnifying glass to see them clearly. Here are some things to look for when you are trying to identify a mineral.

This hematite is black and shiny. It has a lumpy shape.

✱ APPEARANCE: What color is the mineral? Can you see through it, or partly through it? Or is it a solid color? Is it glassy, shiny like metal, or dull and earthy?

✱ SHAPE: What shape is the mineral? Some minerals are shapeless, but others form crystals with definite shapes or break up into a particular pattern.

Iron pyrite often has cube-shaped crystals and looks like silver or gold.

✳ HARDNESS: How hard is the mineral? You can tell by trying to scratch it. You can scratch soft minerals with a copper coin, but you will need a penknife to scratch hard ones. You won't be able to scratch very hard minerals at all.

✳ ROCKS: You can find each mineral in particular kinds of rocks.

These calcite crystals look like quartz, but they are much softer and can be scratched with a penknife.

IRON PYRITE

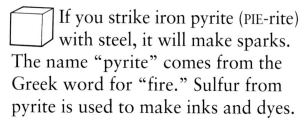 If you strike iron pyrite (PIE-rite) with steel, it will make sparks. The name "pyrite" comes from the Greek word for "fire." Sulfur from pyrite is used to make inks and dyes.

WHERE TO FIND:
You can find iron pyrite throughout North America. It is especially common in Utah and Colorado.

WHAT TO LOOK FOR:

✳ APPEARANCE
Iron pyrite is usually a pale brassy color and has a solid metallic look.

✳ SHAPE
Crystals of iron pyrite are usually shaped like cubes.

✳ HARDNESS
Iron pyrite is too hard to scratch, even with a penknife.

✳ ROCKS
Look for it in rocks, such as granite, that contain a lot of quartz.

The crystals of iron pyrite are usually bright, sparkling cubes.

HEMATITE

If you scratch hematite (HEE-muh-tite) across a white tile or other porcelain surface, you will see a bright red streak. Most of the world's iron comes from hematite.

Hematite sometimes forms round bubbles known as "kidney ore."

WHERE TO FIND:
Good places to look for hematite include the shores of Lake Superior and the Appalachian Mountains.

WHAT TO LOOK FOR:

✳ APPEARANCE
Most hematite is a steel gray color, but it can be reddish, brown, or black. It often looks like a metal.

✳ SHAPE
If you split it open, it forms layers made of fine, needlelike crystals.

✳ HARDNESS
It is very hard and is difficult to scratch.

✳ ROCKS
Sandstone, shale, and limestone can all contain grains of hematite.

○○○○○○○○○○○○○○
FIELD NOTES
People use iron from hematite to make many things, from bridges to pots and pans.

13

QUARTZ

Quartz (KWORTZ) is the most common of the glass minerals, or silicates (SILL-uh-kates). A single crystal of it can weigh as much as 70 tons. Watches and clocks have very thin slices of quartz in them.

Clusters of quartz crystals often look like piles of jewels.

WHERE TO FIND:
Look for quartz almost anywhere in North America. Huge crystals are often found in California.

WHAT TO LOOK FOR:

✷ APPEARANCE
Most quartz is glassy and clear. It can be slightly yellow, pink, brown, or purple, or it can be white and solid.

✷ SHAPE
Crystals are short and pointed. If you fracture them, a rippling pattern forms.

✷ HARDNESS
A penknife will not scratch quartz.

✷ ROCKS
Quartz is in many rocks, including granite and pegmatite.

FIELD NOTES
Purple quartz is called amethyst (AM-uh-thuhst). This beautiful mineral is used to make jewelry.

CALCITE

Stalactites and stalagmites that grow from the roofs and floors of limestone caves are mainly calcite (KAL-site). Calcite looks like quartz but is much softer, and it fizzes if you pour white vinegar on it.

FIELD NOTES

Many seashore creatures, such as periwinkles, mussels, and clams, have shells made of calcite.

Calcite often forms clusters of needlelike crystals. They are called spa.

WHERE TO FIND:
A very common mineral, calcite is found all over North America. Look for crystals in limestone caves.

WHAT TO LOOK FOR:

✳ APPEARANCE
Calcite can be see-through or a solid color. It is often white, but can be tinted yellow, brown, red, or dark gray.

✳ SHAPE
It breaks into diamond-shaped blocks.

✳ HARDNESS
You can easily scratch it with a penknife, and sometimes with a copper coin.

✳ ROCKS
Limestone and marble are made mostly of calcite.

FELDSPAR

Of all the rock-forming minerals on earth, feldspar is the most common. There are two main types: orthoclase (ORE-thoh-klaze) and plagioclase (PLAY-jee-uh-klaze).

Hawaii

WHERE TO FIND:
Feldspar makes up more than half the earth's surface. You can find it in almost all parts of North America.

WHAT TO LOOK FOR:

✳ APPEARANCE
The most common feldspars are white or pink. Some types are clouded and dull, but others are clear and glassy.

✳ SHAPE
Some feldspars form tablet-like crystals.

✳ HARDNESS
You can sometimes scratch feldspar with a penknife.

✳ ROCKS
It is in all types of rocks. The pink mineral in granite is orthoclase feldspar.

Orthoclase feldspar can form beautiful frosty white crystals like these.

○○○○○○○○○○○○○○
FIELD NOTES
Many gemstones
belong to the
feldspar family.
These sunstones
are a kind of
plagioclase.

KAOLINITE

Kaolinite (KAY-uh-luh-nite) feels greasy and smells like clay. It is formed when rain breaks down feldspar. As with other clay minerals, you can mold it when it is wet and it will hold its shape when it dries.

FIELD NOTES

Clay that contains a lot of kaolinite is used to make the world's finest china.

WHERE TO FIND:
You can find kaolinite throughout North America. It will usually be near a deposit of feldspar.

WHAT TO LOOK FOR:

✳ APPEARANCE
It can be white, gray, or yellowish.

✳ SHAPE
Kaolinite has no shape of its own and hardly ever forms crystals.

✳ HARDNESS
Like all clay minerals, kaolinite is very soft. You can scratch it easily with a copper coin, even when it is dry.

✳ ROCKS
Look for kaolinite in igneous rocks such as granite and pegmatite.

Kaolinite often has an earthy look. People use it to make pottery.

MICA

Sheets of mica (MY-kuh) look more like plastic than a mineral. There are two main types: muscovite (MUS-kuh-vite) is white mica, and biotite (BY-uh-tite) is black mica.

WHERE TO FIND:
You can find mica mainly in New Hampshire, North Carolina, South Dakota, Colorado, and Alabama.

WHAT TO LOOK FOR:

✻ APPEARANCE
Mica can be glassy, pearly, or silky. Muscovite is whitish or brownish, but biotite is black or dark green.

✻ SHAPE
Both types split into very thin sheets.

✻ HARDNESS
Mica is so soft that you can scratch it easily with a copper coin.

✻ ROCKS
Look for specks of mica in granite, gneiss, and schist.

Thin plates of brownish muscovite stack up in layers, forming six-sided crystals.

FIELD NOTES

Biotite may form sheets such as these, but you can also see it as the dark flecks in granite.

HORNBLENDE

Most hornblende crystals look like small dark tablets and are scattered through rocks. Sometimes, though, the crystals form in black clusters or in thin, silky fibers.

FIELD NOTES

"Hornblende" is an old German word for the dark part of a rock that miners thought was useless.

WHERE TO FIND:
You can find hornblende in many parts of North America. Look for large crystals in marble deposits.

WHAT TO LOOK FOR:

✳ APPEARANCE
Hornblende is usually glassy, partly see-through, and black or dark green.

✳ SHAPE
The crystals have six sides.

✳ HARDNESS
Hornblende is hard, but you can scratch some kinds with a penknife.

✳ ROCKS
It grows in many light-colored rocks, such as granite, and also in gneiss, schist, and basalt.

Large crystals of hornblende, such as these, are rare and hard to find.

AUGITE

Crystals of augite (AW-jite) look like small squares of dark glass. The lava of many volcanoes is studded with augite crystals. Scientists have even found augite in rocks from the moon!

FIELD NOTES

When volcanoes erupt, they may hurl out augite crystals, along with lots of ash, gas, and lava.

Dark green augite crystals usually grow in rocks that also contain quartz or feldspar.

WHERE TO FIND:
It is found in northeastern and western North America. Look for loose crystals on Hawaiian volcanoes.

WHAT TO LOOK FOR:

✳ APPEARANCE
Augite is a solid black, brown, or greenish black color.

✳ SHAPE
Crystals are usually small. They can be squarish or eight-sided.

✳ HARDNESS
Augite is hard, but you can scratch some types with a penknife.

✳ ROCKS
Augite grows in dark igneous rocks such as gabbro, basalt, and tuff.

27

OLIVINE

The name "olivine" (OLL-uh-veen) comes from this mineral's olive green color. It usually looks like tiny pieces of broken glass. Sometimes crystals form in the hollows of rocks.

Hawaii

WHERE TO FIND:
Look for it in mountains throughout North America, especially in North Carolina, Arizona, and New Mexico.

WHAT TO LOOK FOR:

✳ APPEARANCE
Olivine is usually green and glassy. It can be see-through or cloudy.

✳ SHAPE
It often forms small round crystals. If you strike it, it forms a pattern that looks like ripples in a pond.

✳ HARDNESS
You cannot scratch olivine, even with a penknife.

✳ ROCKS
Look for it in dark rocks such as basalt.

Olivine sometimes makes a green, sugary coating on a rock.

FIELD NOTES

Some crystals of olivine are large and clear. These can be cut into gemstones called peridot.

LOOKING AT ROCKS

Most rocks you see have been exposed to the weather for a long time. They have been worn down by wind and rain and their surfaces have become dirty.

The best way to investigate a rock is by cracking it open with a small hammer so that you can look at a clean, fresh surface. But this can be dangerous! Ask an adult to help you break the rock—and make sure you are wearing safety goggles.

Now you can closely examine the rock. Use a magnifying glass to see more detail.

The weather can carve sandstone into remarkable shapes, such as this boulder.

Here are some features to look for:

✳ **COLORS**: You can sometimes identify a rock by its color, or colors. But keep in mind that rocks can be stained by minerals that are not usually in them.

Sandstone and other sedimentary rocks often have layers of different colors.

✳ **GRAIN SIZE**: The minerals and/or bits of other rocks that make up a rock are called grains. How big are these grains? Are they round or pointed? Are they all the same size? Can you see any crystals in the rock?

✳ **COMPOSITION**: How many kinds of minerals can you see in the rock? Are there fossils—that is, the remains of animals or plants—or bits of other rocks inside it?

✳ **PATTERNS**: Can you see any patterns, such as layers, in the rock? When you hit it with a hammer, does it break up in a particular way?

When you break obsidian, it forms a ripple-like pattern.

BASALT

Basalt started out as magma that flowed from a volcano. All ocean floors are made of basalt, but it is less common on land. Sometimes basalt is crushed and used in concrete.

WHERE TO FIND:
You can find basalt in North America's East and West. Look along the Columbia River in Washington State.

Hawaii

WHAT TO LOOK FOR:

✴ COLORS
Fresh basalt is very dark blue-gray or black. Weathered basalt often has a bright red, dusty coating.

✴ GRAIN SIZE
You might see some olivine crystals, but most grains are too small to see.

✴ COMPOSITION
It can contain feldspar, augite, iron minerals, and sometimes a little olivine.

✴ PATTERNS
Basalt can form six-sided columns.

The small pits in these basalt boulders
were made by bubbles of gas in the magma.

○○○○○○○○○○○○○○
FIELD NOTES
The Devil's Tower,
in Wyoming,
is made up
of hundreds
of basalt
columns.

GABBRO

The mineral crystals in gabbro grew over millions of years as magma, deep under the ground, cooled slowly. This is why gabbro has larger grains than basalt, even though it has similar ingredients.

These large, flat boulders of gabbro are in the Adirondack Mountains, in New York.

WHAT TO LOOK FOR:

✳ **COLORS**
Gabbro is usually dark gray and often has a greenish tint.

✳ **GRAIN SIZE**
The grains of gabbro are medium size and easy to see.

✳ **COMPOSITION**
It usually has feldspar in it. You might also see some augite or olivine and a tiny amount of mica or hornblende.

✳ **PATTERNS**
Gabbro has a rough, grainy surface.

RHYOLITE

Rhyolite (RYE-uh-lite), like basalt, began as magma from a volcano. But the magma that formed rhyolite was sticky, and did not flow. You can sometimes see rhyolite inside large cracks in other rocks.

Wind and rain slowly wore away thick beds of cooled magma to create these towers of rhyolite.

WHAT TO LOOK FOR:

✳ COLORS
Rhyolite can be reddish brown, or pale gray, pink, or yellow.

✳ GRAIN SIZE
The grain is very fine, but you might see larger crystals of feldspar.

✳ COMPOSITION
It contains lots of feldspar and quartz, and sometimes a little mica or augite.

✳ PATTERNS
Rhyolite is often banded. It sometimes has small bubbles with crystals inside.

FIELD NOTES

The bands in this rhyolite were made when tiny crystals moved around in the magma.

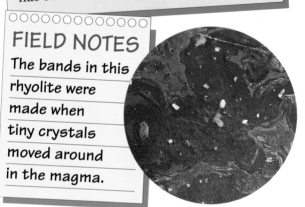

37

OBSIDIAN

 You can recognize obsidian (ub-SID-ee-uhn) by its smooth, glassy surface. It is a kind of rhyolite that formed when magma cooled so quickly that crystals could not grow.

WHERE TO FIND:
There are large deposits of obsidian in California, New Mexico, and Oregon. Look for it near rhyolite deposits.

WHAT TO LOOK FOR:

✳ COLORS
Obsidian is usually black, but it can be green or light brown.

✳ GRAIN SIZE
You cannot see any grain in obsidian, even through a strong microscope.

✳ COMPOSITION
Like rhyolite, it has lots of feldspar and quartz and may have mica or augite.

✳ PATTERNS
Obsidian breaks into curved, clean surfaces with round-shaped ripples.

These shiny, black cliffs of obsidian are in Oregon. The rock on top is rhyolite.

○○○○○○○○○○○○○

FIELD NOTES

In ancient times, some people carved masks and made sharp arrowheads from obsidian.

PUMICE

When rhyolite magma has lots of gas in it, it becomes frothy and forms pumice (PUM-uhs). Because of the gas bubbles inside it, pumice is very light. It is the only rock that can float in water.

FIELD NOTES

People often use pieces of pumice to rub away bits of hard, coarse skin on their feet and elbows.

Pumice that you find on a beach may have come from a volcano thousands of miles away.

WHERE TO FIND:
There is a lot of pumice in the Rocky Mountains, but you may also find it washed up on West Coast beaches.

WHAT TO LOOK FOR:

✳ COLORS
Most pumice is medium gray, but it can also be pinkish or brown.

✳ GRAIN SIZE
Most grains in pumice are too small to see, even through a magnifying glass.

✳ COMPOSITION
Pumice is a type of rhyolite and is mostly feldspar and quartz.

✳ PATTERNS
Bubbles of gas in pumice give it a honeycomb look.

TUFF

When sand, dust, and ash from a volcano settle on the ground, they can cover large areas and turn into beds of tuff (TUHF). Sometimes tuff forms from tiny pieces of ash that have been blown thousands of miles.

Because tuff is soft, wind and rain can quickly mold it into rounded shapes.

WHERE TO FIND:
You will find tuff, often in large flat sheets, in western North America, especially in parts of Montana.

WHAT TO LOOK FOR:

✳ **COLORS**
Tuff is sometimes white or pinkish, but it is usually gray.

✳ **GRAIN SIZE**
Grains can be as big as sand grains or as tiny as grains of very fine dust.

✳ **COMPOSITION**
Look for tiny pieces of pumice, crystals of feldspar or quartz, and splinters of glass.

✳ **PATTERNS**
Tuff has layers that are easy to see.

○○○○○○○○○○○○
FIELD NOTES
When animals are caught in tuff, their shape is sometimes preserved in the rock.

GRANITE

 When magma cools very slowly deep inside mountains, granite (GRAN-uht) forms. This hard rock is a very popular building stone. It looks very shiny when it is polished.

WHERE TO FIND:
Granite can be found in the mountains of the East and West. Look in Yosemite National Park, in California.

WHAT TO LOOK FOR:

✷ COLORS
Most granite is light gray or pink.

✷ GRAIN SIZE
Granite has a fairly large grain. Its crystals are easy to see.

✷ COMPOSITION
About one-third of a piece of granite is quartz. Granite also contains lots of feldspar and some mica or hornblende.

✷ PATTERNS
When it breaks, its surfaces are rough and grainy.

Granite usually forms rounded boulders, but it can also be sharp and craggy.

FIELD NOTES
In this granite, you can see pink and white feldspar, clear quartz, and black biotite mica and hornblende.

PEGMATITE

If a granite magma cools very slowly over millions of years, the crystals will grow very large and form pegmatite (PEG-muh-tite). A pegmatite crystal can grow as large as an adult person.

FIELD NOTES

In some types of pegmatite, you can see crystals of rare minerals such as topaz and gold.

WHERE TO FIND:
There is pegmatite in the mountains of the East and West. You are most likely to find it near granite.

WHAT TO LOOK FOR:

* **COLORS**
It is usually white, pale gray, or pink.

* **GRAIN SIZE**
Crystals in pegmatite are always large and very easy to see.

* **COMPOSITION**
Like granite, pegmatite contains lots of quartz, feldspar, and biotite mica, as well as other minerals.

* **PATTERNS**
Sometimes different types of minerals cluster together into zones.

The wind and rain can shape pegmatite into rounded boulders like these.

SANDSTONE

Over time, minerals dissolved in water can cement together sand grains. This creates a rock called sandstone. Most sandstone begins in rivers, but it can also form in the sea, on beaches, and in desert dunes.

You often see stripe patterns, like these, in sandstone. They are called crossbeds.

WHERE TO FIND:
Sandstone is a common rock, especially in the West. The Grand Canyon is made of sandstone.

WHAT TO LOOK FOR:

✳ COLORS
Sandstone can be yellow, red, gray, or more rarely, white.

✳ GRAIN SIZE
Grains vary in size but you can see them all clearly.

✳ COMPOSITION
Most sandstone grains are quartz.

✳ PATTERNS
The patterns in sandstone are made by flowing water. They include ripple marks and different-colored layers.

FIELD NOTES
Wind and rain can wear away sandstone until it forms shapes like this arch.

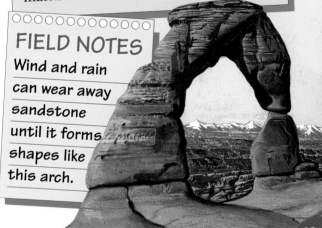

CONGLOMERATE

When rounded rock fragments are cemented together by minerals, they make conglomerate (kuhn-GLOM-uh-ruht). This rock can form in streams, on coral reefs, or in places where glaciers used to be.

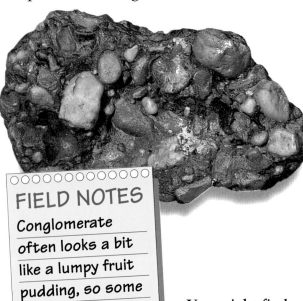

FIELD NOTES

Conglomerate often looks a bit like a lumpy fruit pudding, so some people call it puddingstone!

You might find conglomerate on rocky shores near the ocean.

WHERE TO FIND:
There are huge deposits of conglomerate in Death Valley, in California, and in Van Horn, in Texas.

WHAT TO LOOK FOR:

✳ COLORS
It can have many colors in it, but it is mainly red, yellow, and gray.

✳ GRAIN SIZE
Most grains are larger than sand grains. Some can be bigger than your fist.

✳ COMPOSITION
Look for fragments of other rocks, especially granite, quartzite, and flint.

✳ PATTERNS
Larger grains are usually at the bottom, with smaller grains on top.

MUDSTONE

 When mud collects on an ocean floor, a lake bed, or another place where water moves slowly, it can turn into mudstone. This rock is usually soft and breaks up easily.

WHERE TO FIND:
You can find mudstone mainly in central North America, and in the Painted Desert, in Arizona.

WHAT TO LOOK FOR:

✳ **COLORS**
Mudstone can be red, brown, yellow, gray, or white.

✳ **GRAIN SIZE**
You need a magnifying glass to see the tiny particles of clay in it.

✳ **COMPOSITION**
Look for fine grains of quartz, as well as feldspar, mica, and clay minerals.

✳ **PATTERNS**
Most mudstone forms into thick layers of different colors.

Wind and rain sometimes shape mudstone into low, rounded hills with steep sides.

FIELD NOTES

Mudstone is used to make bricks and roof tiles for houses, as well as pots for houseplants.

SHALE

Shale is a very fine-grained rock that splits into thin, flaky layers. It forms in still waters at the bottom of deep lakes or in the depths of the ocean. Oil and tar come from some kinds of shale.

Yellow stains in shale are made by iron minerals. Tiny plants can cause green stains.

WHERE TO FIND:
Shale is found mainly in central North America. Miners drill it for oil in Utah, Wyoming, and other places.

WHAT TO LOOK FOR:

✳ **COLORS**
Shale is usually dark gray or black.

✳ **GRAIN SIZE**
You need a magnifying glass to see most of the grains in shale.

✳ **COMPOSITION**
Shale contains quartz, mica, and other minerals.

✳ **PATTERNS**
Look closely at shale and you will see very fine layers.

FIELD NOTES

People sometimes find well-preserved fossils of plants and animals in fine layers of shale.

55

PEAT

When dead plants collect in still water, they sometimes slowly bind together to form peat. The plant material in peat is what gives this dark, spongy rock its often "boggy" smell.

FIELD NOTES

In some parts of the world, people burn peat to heat their houses and cook food.

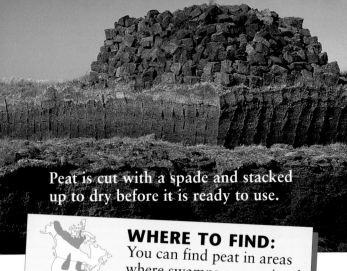

Peat is cut with a spade and stacked
up to dry before it is ready to use.

WHERE TO FIND:

You can find peat in areas
where swamps once existed,
including Utah, Minnesota,
and northern Canada.

WHAT TO LOOK FOR:

✳ **COLORS**

Peat is dark brown to black.

✳ **GRAIN SIZE**

You may be able to see some grains
of quartz or other minerals in peat.

✳ **COMPOSITION**

Peat is mostly carbon—a mineral that
comes from dead plants—and water.

✳ **PATTERNS**

Peat sometimes has rough layers of
compressed plants in it. You can split
it along these layers.

COAL

When rocks press down on peat, they dry it out and make it harder, turning it into coal. A peat bed one hundred feet thick can be squashed to less than one foot of coal.

FIELD NOTES

Most of the world's electricity comes from coal, which is burned in large power stations.

You often see coal between beds of mudstone or shale.

WHERE TO FIND:
There are large deposits of coal in Pennsylvania, West Virginia, Utah, Illinois, and the Mississippi Valley.

WHAT TO LOOK FOR:

✳ COLORS
Softer kinds of coal are earthy brown. Harder kinds are black.

✳ GRAIN SIZE
You can rarely see any grain in coal, but you may see silt or specks of minerals.

✳ COMPOSITION
Like peat, coal is mostly black carbon, but it contains much less water.

✳ PATTERNS
Hard, black coal has sharp-edged, shiny surfaces.

LIMESTONE

 Most limestone forms on the seafloor, where the minerals in seawater bind together grains of sand and pieces of shell. Cement for buildings comes from limestone.

WHERE TO FIND:
Limestone is widespread all around the world. Much of central Texas is made of limestone.

WHAT TO LOOK FOR:

✳ COLORS
It is usually blue-gray, but if you break it open it can be yellow, orange, or white.

✳ GRAIN SIZE
Grains vary from gravel-size ones to very fine grains that you cannot see.

✳ COMPOSITION
Limestone contains lots of calcite. You can sometimes find broken shells and even fossils in it.

✳ PATTERNS
It often has a sugary or glassy texture.

The weather can turn limestone from pale yellow or gray to a darker steel gray.

○○○○○○○○○○○○○
FIELD NOTES
Mild natural acids
dissolve limestone
in caves, forming
hanging stalactites
and standing
stalagmites.

CHERT AND FLINT

The skeletons of billions of tiny sea creatures can collect on the seafloor and turn into chert or flint. Chert often forms thick beds deep in the ocean. Sometimes flint takes the shape of old animal burrows.

FIELD NOTES

In prehistoric times, people chipped flint to make arrowheads for hunting.

You might find pebbles of chert in streams.

WHERE TO FIND:
Chert is found mainly in eastern and western North America, while flint is found in the central region.

WHAT TO LOOK FOR:

✳ COLORS
Chert and flint can be white, gray, brown, or black.

✳ GRAIN SIZE
Even through a magnifying glass, you can't see any crystals in chert or flint.

✳ COMPOSITION
Chert and flint are made of silica minerals similar to quartz.

✳ PATTERNS
Both rocks are very hard. They break into curved surfaces with round ripples.

GNEISS

Deep beneath the ground, movements in the earth create heat and pressure that can turn rocks such as granite into gneiss (NICE). The name "gneiss" comes from a German word that means "sparkling."

This canyon in New Mexico has walls of black and white gneiss.

WHERE TO FIND:
You can find gneiss in some mountain ranges. There are large amounts of it in Idaho and New York.

WHAT TO LOOK FOR:

✱ COLORS
Like granite, gneiss is usually gray or pink. It can have dark streaks or layers.

✱ GRAIN SIZE
The grains in gneiss are large enough to see without using a magnifying glass.

✱ COMPOSITION
The light-colored bands are mainly quartz and feldspar. The dark minerals include mica and hornblende.

✱ PATTERNS
Gneiss forms a rough, craggy landscape.

000000000000000

FIELD NOTES

You can easily recognize gneiss by the wavy bands of light and dark minerals.

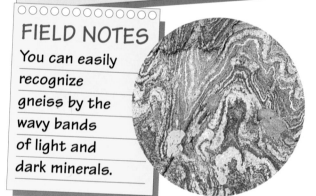

SCHIST

When basalt or shale changes deep below the earth's surface, it turns into schist (SHIST). Schist looks like gneiss, but it has much thinner bands of minerals. It is flaky and crumbles like crisp pastry.

FIELD NOTES

Sometimes beautifully formed crystals of garnet are found in pieces of schist.

These hills in Idaho are made of schist. Notice the glossy sheen on the plates on the ground.

WHERE TO FIND:
You are most likely to find schist in mountain ranges. There is a lot of schist in Idaho and California.

WHAT TO LOOK FOR:

✳ COLORS
It varies from greenish or bluish gray to greenish black. It can also be white.

✳ GRAIN SIZE
The grains are large and easy to see.

✳ COMPOSITION
Look for silky plates of muscovite or biotite mica in wavy layers. There might also be some quartz and feldspar.

✳ PATTERNS
Most schist has a shiny, sparkling look and feels very smooth.

SLATE

As mountains form, shale or mudstone may be squeezed so much that it turns into slate. This hard stone is not easily worn away by wind and rain.

FIELD NOTES

Because it forms smooth, hard plates, slate is a good material for roof tiles.

Slate looks similar to shale, but it splits into smooth sheets.

WHERE TO FIND:
You can find slate in old mountain ranges such as the Rockies, in the West, and the Appalachians, in the East.

WHAT TO LOOK FOR:

✳ COLORS
Most slate is black or dark gray. Small amounts of iron minerals can create patterns of reds, yellows, and browns.

✳ GRAIN SIZE
Its grain is too fine to see, even through a magnifying glass.

✳ COMPOSITION
Slate has lots of quartz and mica in it.

✳ PATTERNS
Slate splits along layers where the mica grains have lined up.

MARBLE

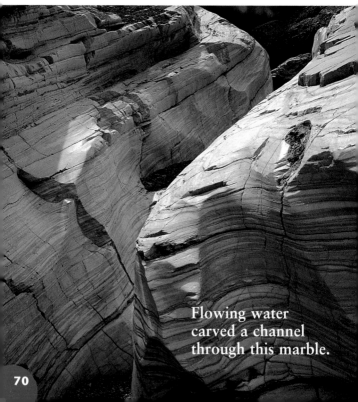

Marble forms as mountains are building up and limestone is squeezed and heated. Since ancient times, people have used marble for buildings and statues. It is a hard rock, but it can be carved.

Flowing water carved a channel through this marble.

70

WHERE TO FIND:
You are most likely to see marble in mountain areas, usually near a deposit of schist or gneiss.

WHAT TO LOOK FOR:

✳ COLORS
Pure marble is white, but it is often stained brown, red, yellow, or green.

✳ GRAIN SIZE
You can see calcite crystals in some marble, but often the crystals are joined together and hard to see.

✳ COMPOSITION
Marble is mainly calcite.

✳ PATTERNS
The texture of marble can be sugary or smooth.

FIELD NOTES

Traces of minerals, in addition to calcite, often produce colorful swirling patterns in marble.

QUARTZITE

Heat and pressure deep inside the earth, or hot magma on the surface, can turn sandstone into quartzite (KWORT-zite). Because it is hard, quartzite resists the weather and often forms cliffs and ledges.

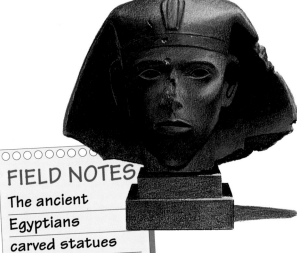

FIELD NOTES

The ancient Egyptians carved statues out of quartzite, like this one of a pharaoh, or king.

Quartzite does not make good soil. You usually find it in rocky, barren places.

WHERE TO FIND:
You are most likely to find quartzite near the bottom of old mountain chains or near deposits of granite.

WHAT TO LOOK FOR:

✳ COLORS
Pure quartzite is white, but it is often stained red, green, gray, or yellow.

✳ GRAIN SIZE
Single grains are hard to see because they have been heated into a glassy or sugary mass.

✳ COMPOSITION
Quartzite is almost entirely quartz.

✳ PATTERNS
You may be able to see the layers of the original sandstone.

METEORITES

 When a shooting star lands on earth, it is called a meteorite (MEET-ee-uh-rite). The largest known meteorite weighs over 65 tons, but most are little and as light as pebbles.

WHERE TO FIND:
You could find a meteorite anywhere in the world, but they are very rare. Most land in oceans or deserts.

WHAT TO LOOK FOR:

✳ COLORS
As a meteorite hurtles through the earth's atmosphere, its outside turns black. Inside, it can be brown or silver.

✳ GRAIN SIZE
Different meteorites have different-size grains. Some have no grains at all.

✳ COMPOSITION
Some are made mostly of augite and olivine. Others are solid metal.

✳ PATTERNS
Look for melted patterns on the surface.

Meteor Crater, in Arizona, is almost a mile wide. It was made by a huge meteorite.

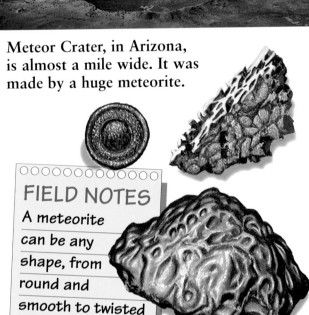

FIELD NOTES

A meteorite can be any shape, from round and smooth to twisted and pitted.

GLOSSARY

Ancient Belonging to a time in early history.

Banding Where you can see stripes of different minerals in a rock.

Boulder A large, rounded rock.

Composition The substances that make up a rock or mineral.

Compressed Being squashed or squeezed.

Crystal The shape in which a mineral occurs in nature.

Deposit A mass of rock or mineral in the ground.

Fossil The remains of a plant or animal that have turned to stone.

Fracture To break a rock or mineral.

Gemstone A precious stone that can be cut and polished into a jewel.

Glacier A huge sheet of ice that covers land.

Igneous rock A rock that formed from cooled magma.

Lava Hot, liquid rock, or magma, that flows from a volcano.

Magma Rock that has melted and turned into a liquid.

Metamorphic rock A rock that has been changed by being heated or squeezed.

Mineral A natural, non-living substance.

Prehistoric Belonging to a time before people recorded history in writing.

Preserved Protected against decay or damage.

Rock A solid mass made of minerals or rock fragments that occurs in nature.

Sedimentary rock A rock that formed from bits of other rocks or plants.

Stalactite A cone-shaped rock that hangs from a cave roof. It forms as dissolved limestone drips from the roof.

Stalagmite A cone-shaped rock standing on the floor of a cave. It forms as dissolved limestone drips from the roof.

Tint Where a rock or mineral has been colored naturally.

Volcano A place on the surface of the earth, usually a mountain, where magma comes out.

INDEX OF
MINERALS

ROCKS

PHOTOGRAPHIC CREDITS

The world's largest nonprofit scientific and educational organization, the National Geographic Society was founded in 1888 "for the increase and diffusion of geographic knowledge." Since then it has supported scientific exploration and spread information to its more than eight million members worldwide.

The National Geographic Society educates and inspires millions every day through magazines, books, television programs, videos, maps and atlases, research grants, the National Geographic Bee, teacher workshops, and innovative classroom materials.

The Society is supported through membership dues, charitable gifts, and income from the sale of its educational products.

Members receive NATIONAL GEOGRAPHIC magazine—the Society's official journal— discounts on Society products, and other benefits.

For more information about the National Geographic Society, its educational programs, publications, or ways to support its work, please call 1-800-NGS-LINE (647-5463), or write to the following address:

National Geographic Society
1145 17th Street, N.W.
Washington, D.C. 20036-4688 U.S.A.

Visit the Society's Web site: www.nationalgeographic.com

FIELD NOTES

FIELD NOTES

SKETCHES

FIELD NOTES

SKETCHES

FIELD NOTES

SKETCHES

FIELD NOTES

SKETCHES

FIELD NOTES

SKETCHES

FIELD NOTES

SKETCHES

FIELD NOTES